MINDFULNESS WORKBOOK FOR KIDS

MINDFULNESS
WORKBOOK for KIDS
For Ages 8–12

60+
Activities to Focus, Stay Calm,
and Make Good Choices

Hannah Sherman, LCSW

Illustrated by Sarah Rebar

ROCKRIDGE
PRESS

Interior and Cover Designer: Scott Petrower
Art Producer: Karen Williams
Editor: Samantha Barbaro
Illustration © 2020 Sarah Rebar. Author photo courtesy of © Jacquelyn Potter.

ISBN: Print 978-1-64739-675-6 | eBook 978-1-64739-399-1
R0

This book is dedicated to every child I've worked with
who has inspired me to navigate each day with a
curious and kind heart, and to Celia Rose, who led the path
for us all to do fancy things for the world.

Contents

A Letter to Kids

Hello, and welcome!

My name is Hannah, and I work at a school and private practice in Brooklyn, New York. Every day I work with kids to help them develop the tools they need to deal with tough situations and difficult emotions. What I love most about my job is being able to teach kids about the power of mindfulness! Mindfulness is a practice that helps you become aware of what is happening inside and outside of your body. It also helps you accept your experiences as they are instead of trying to push them away or thinking that they're wrong. Through mindfulness, you learn to be kinder to yourself and the people around you.

During my years of working with kids and teenagers (and using mindfulness practices myself), I've been able to see the ways mindfulness can help us overcome challenging situations, take care of big feelings, and learn from our experiences and the world around us.

This workbook is intended to help you start your own mindfulness journey! It is filled with mindfulness practices and activities that will help you create a stronger connection to yourself and the world around you. The practices and activities will help you learn to deal with the different experiences and challenges all kids face with curiosity and compassion. My hope is that this workbook gives you an opportunity to reflect, grow, and learn.

As you explore the activities in this workbook, you will become more tuned in to your feelings, thoughts, and behaviors. You will learn mindfulness tools that will help you start your day on the right foot, work through difficult emotions, and make better decisions. These mindfulness tools will also help you find your focus, face your worries, act with kindness toward yourself and others, and end your day on a positive note.

It is important that you start by reading the first chapter, which is all about how mindfulness works and how it can help you. After that, you can go through the workbook from start to finish or skip around to different chapters that look interesting to you. Maybe you want to pay better attention in school—go right to chapter 3. If you want to learn how to handle your worries, go to chapter 5. This is your journey, and this book is here to help guide you along the way. Are you ready? Let's get started!

A Letter to Grown-Ups

Welcome, parents and guardians!

I'm so excited for your child (or student) to start their mindfulness journey! What does it mean to be mindful, anyway? Mindfulness means being aware of your internal and external experience without judging it. I discovered the immense value of mindfulness as a pathway to healing and growth when I first started my clinical work with children and adolescents. Today, one of my greatest passions is supporting children and their families with incorporating mindfulness-based practices into their everyday lives.

I've been able to witness the range of benefits mindfulness has on the lives of children across development in my work in various settings, including mental health clinics, schools, and private practice. Mindfulness helps support and celebrate children's inherent curiosity about themselves and the world around them. The list of benefits of mindfulness for youth continues to grow; it includes improved focus and concentration, greater ability to self-regulate, and development of a positive sense of self. All of these benefits help children manage symptoms of many of the most common mental health challenges kids experience, including ADHD, depression, and anxiety-related disorders. Overall, mindfulness helps children establish a positive connection to their bodies and feel empowered by their minds.

This workbook offers children ages eight to twelve an introduction to mindfulness and the many different ways to practice it. In this book, you'll find 62 exercises that will help kids understand their feelings, apply focus, manage difficult emotions, stay calm when things get tough, and be kind to themselves and others. I encourage you to read along with them and invite them to share with you what they're learning along the way! Many of these practices are a wonderful way to connect with your children and support their mindfulness journey.

CHAPTER 1

THE BUILDING BLOCKS OF MINDFULNESS

Welcome to your mindfulness journey! In this chapter, you'll learn all about mindfulness, including what it is, why it's helpful, and how to use it as a practice. You'll use your senses to listen to your breath, your body, and the world around you.

What Is Mindfulness?

Mindfulness helps you become aware of what's happening inside and outside of your body. *Mindful awareness* means being aware of what you're experiencing in this moment and accepting it as it is, without trying to push the experience away or thinking that it's wrong. Mindfulness can help you be kinder to yourself and to the people around you. You can explore mindfulness in lots of different ways, including breathing practices, meditation, movement, and art activities.

Sometimes when we hear the word *mindfulness*, we think of feeling calm and relaxed. Mindfulness can certainly help us feel this way! But it's important to remember that mindfulness is a practice—it's something we do with our awareness. It's not a feeling or a way to be. We can always become more mindful (or aware) of our own experiences and the world around us. In this way, mindfulness is about making progress, not about becoming a master or super-champion! Mindfulness is not a race or a competition. It's about trying different practices and finding out what works for you.

Mindfulness Can Help with So Much!

Maybe you're thinking to yourself, *"Why should I care about mindfulness, anyway?"* For starters, mindfulness makes it easier to listen to yourself. By using mindfulness, you'll be able to better hear what your mind and body want to say to you. This is helpful in so many ways!

Mindfulness helps you be kind to yourself and to others, including your friends and family. It helps you build confidence and feel good about who you are. It can also help you control how you react to different feelings and experiences, even the really tough ones. It can help you stop and take a breath when you're feeling angry and think about what you want to say to your friend when you're feeling sad. Mindfulness also helps you pause and think before you act. This makes it easier to solve problems and make good choices, instead of choices you'll be sorry about later.

Mindfulness helps you start your day on a good foot, and it helps you calm down and sleep well at night. Mindfulness helps you all day long!

MINDFULNESS CHECK-IN

The statements below are about everyday situations at home and at school. Circle how often you experience each situation. (Don't be afraid to be honest—this is a judgment-free zone!)

After reading a page of a book, I can't remember what I just read about.

Always   **Sometimes**   **Never**

My teacher gives directions in class and I don't know what to do because I was thinking about something else.

Always   **Sometimes**   **Never**

My sad or angry feelings sometimes get bottled up because I try to avoid feeling them.

Always   **Sometimes**   **Never**

I quickly move from one task to another, often without finishing the first task.

Always   **Sometimes**   **Never**

When I'm mad or frustrated, I say things or yell without thinking.

Always   **Sometimes**   **Never**

I interrupt a friend when they're telling me a story.

Always   **Sometimes**   **Never**

I spend most of my time thinking about things that happened in the past or will happen in the future.

Always   **Sometimes**   **Never**

Take a moment to look over and think about your responses. Are you surprised by any of your answers? Did you notice anything about yourself? Mindfulness can help with all of the situations described here. Come back to this exercise as often as you want during your mindfulness journey as a way to check in with yourself. (Hint: The less often these situations occur, the more mindful awareness you're experiencing!)

Be Mindful Anytime, Anywhere

Mindfulness is like a magical power that is available to you at any moment. You get to choose when and how to use it!

You can be mindful of what is happening *internally*, or inside of your body. This includes your thoughts, breath, and body. You can also be mindful of what's happening *externally*, or outside of your body. These are the things occurring in the environment around you.

Here comes the fun part: You can practice being mindful of all of these things in many different ways! You can explore mindfulness through meditation (deep, focused thinking) or reflection (quiet time with your thoughts). You can also explore mindfulness through movement and art. Perhaps most important, you can practice mindfulness by simply taking a moment to notice what's going on inside and out.

This workbook will introduce you to dozens of different mindfulness activities. Try them all! Afterward, you can repeat the activities you enjoyed the most and the ones you found were most helpful to you.

Your Thoughts

Have you ever noticed your own thoughts? Imagine your thoughts as being like ocean waves at the beach. Thoughts come, and thoughts go. Some are big and powerful, while others are small and gentle. Some thoughts are loud and drown out everything else, while others are quiet and hard to hear. It might be easy to notice your thoughts at certain times, like when you're alone. But it might be tough to notice them at other times, such as when you're hanging out with your friends.

We all experience different types of thoughts, including positive thoughts and negative thoughts. Thoughts are often connected to different emotions. Listening to your thoughts can help you understand which thoughts are connected to certain feelings and events. But we need to be alert, because sometimes our thoughts tell us things that aren't necessarily true. Just read this story about Pilar:

> *Pilar noticed she was feeling sad after arguing with a friend. After taking a moment to notice her thoughts, she realized that the thought* **"Nobody cares about me"** *kept popping into her head. Pilar recognized that this was a negative thought. Once she was able to label the thought, the thought didn't have as much power. She also realized it wasn't true. Whenever she noticed herself thinking in a negative way, she asked herself, "Am I jumping to a big conclusion right now? Is there another way to look at what happened?" Labeling her thoughts and changing how she saw them helped Pilar understand them and turned the fight with her friend into a learning experience.*

BIG THOUGHTS, LITTLE THOUGHTS

Take a moment and close your eyes. Bring your attention to your mind. What thoughts do you notice? Are they big and powerful, like giant waves at the beach? Or are they small and gentle, like little waves?

Write down the thoughts you notice below.

GIANT WAVES

LITTLE WAVES

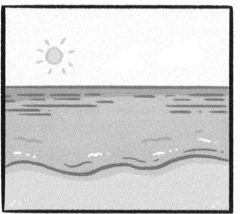

Your Breath

One of the most powerful things we can be mindful of is our own breath. Our bodies breathe in many different ways. For instance, our breathing can be fast and shallow or slow and deep. Being aware of your own breath can help you notice what you are feeling and what you might need. The way you're breathing can tell you how you're feeling in both your mind and your body.

Otis noticed that when he feels anxious, he breathes really fast in and out through his mouth. It's like he just ran a race and needs to get more air. When this happens, Otis finds it very hard to control his breathing. He decided to start bringing his attention to his breath when he feels anxious. He does this by inhaling through his nose as he counts to four. Then he exhales through his mouth as he counts to four. Doing this over and over helps Otis control his breathing and calm down.

FEELING YOUR BREATH

Start by putting one hand on your belly and one hand on your heart. Take a moment to notice your breath, but don't try to change it. Can you feel your breath in your body? Where do you feel your breath when you inhale? Where do you feel it when you exhale? Circle all of the words that describe your breath right now.

Shallow

Easy

Deep

Difficult

Heavy

Quick

Light

Slow

Your Body

You've practiced being mindful of your thoughts and your breath, which can help you better understand your experiences and feelings. Now we're going to explore what it means to be mindful of your whole body! The connection between the mind and the body reminds us that our thoughts, feelings, and behaviors are all related.

Being aware of your body means noticing how your body feels. When you're feeling happy, your body might feel calm and focused. When you're feeling frustrated, your body might feel busy or distracted, and you might make sudden movements. By being mindful of the different signals your body is sending you, you become more aware of how you're feeling. By being more aware, you become better able to take care of yourself.

HOW DOES MY BODY FEEL?

This activity is a body scan practice, which will help you notice sensations coming from different parts of your body. Doing the scan allows you to check in with how your body is feeling. Start by bringing your awareness to your toes and feet. Focus on them. How do your toes and feet feel in this moment? Do you notice any physical sensations? For instance, do your feet feel warm or cold? See if you can feel your feet touching the ground. Next, bring your awareness up to your legs. How do your legs feel? Are they moving around or are they still and calm? Now bring your awareness to your belly. How is your belly feeling? Is it hungry or full? Bring your awareness to your hands and arms. Notice where your hands are resting. Feel the weight of your arms next to you. Next, bring your awareness to your back, chest, and shoulders. Are you feeling relaxed or tense? Are you sitting up straight and tall, or are you slouching forward? Keep going. Bring your awareness all the way up to the top of your head. Does your head feel light or heavy? Overall, does your body feel busy or calm?

Using colors and words, show and say how your body feels at this moment.

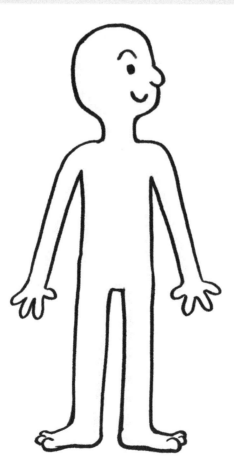

Your Environment

Have you ever walked to the store or a friend's house, and when you arrived you realized that you didn't notice anything around you during your walk? Your mind was on other things, and you could barely remember how you got there!

Mindfulness helps you develop a deeper connection to yourself. But it can also help you feel more connected to the world around you. Most important, mindfulness reminds you to appreciate your journey through this world.

Paying more attention to your five senses can help you stay connected to your environment. (Do you remember what the five senses are? They are touch, sight, hearing, smell, and taste.) When you're more aware of your senses, you can pay better attention to your surroundings and notice what's going on around you. For example, on your walk to school you might hear the sounds of cars passing by or see someone walking their dog.

3-2-1: TUNING IN TO YOUR SENSES

To begin this activity, take in the environment you're in at this moment. Notice what you see around you. Next, notice any sounds you hear, including sounds that are close and far away. Finally, notice what you are touching or feeling at this moment. Can you feel the ground under your feet? Can you feel the chair you're sitting on or the clothes on your body?

Write down 3 things you see at this moment.

....

....

....

Write down 2 things you hear at this moment.

....

....

Write down 1 thing you are touching at this moment.

....

All Together Now!

You now know all the different ways you can use mindfulness. But you don't have to use all the practices all the time! You can choose which practices to use and when to use them. Mindfulness is a tool you can use at any time. You can be mindful at home, at school, when you're alone, or when you're with other people. Try exploring all of the different ways to use mindfulness. By doing that, you can figure out which practices work best for you.

How can you know which mindfulness practice might be helpful at a certain moment? One good way to figure that out is by asking yourself this question: *"What do I need right now?"* For example, if you notice that your body is feeling busy at school and it's hard to pay attention in class, try a breathing practice. If you notice that you're feeling sleepy in the morning, try a practice that involves movement to wake your body up. When you know all of the different ways you can use mindfulness throughout the day, you'll be ready to take care of yourself all day long!

MY MINDFULNESS TOOLBOX

Try thinking about everything you've learned and done in this chapter. You've learned to notice your big and little thoughts, and you've learned to feel your breath in your body. You've done a body scan, and you've tuned in to your senses. So far, which practices do you like best? Which ones do you think are most helpful to you? Why? Write your answers on the lines below.

....

....

....

....

....

....

....

Think about the things you do every day, like waking up, going to school, taking tests, talking to your friends or siblings, playing games, and getting ready for bed. Do you think mindfulness could be helpful with any of these situations? Which ones? For example, tuning in to your senses at school might help you stay focused and calm when you're doing your classroom work. Maybe doing a breathing practice at night would help you relax and get to sleep. Write down the situations where you think mindfulness would be helpful.

....

....

....

....

....

....

Think about when you might be able to use mindfulness during your day. In the spaces below, write down your favorite mindfulness practices.

MORNING

....

....

....

....

....

....

AT SCHOOL

....

....

....

....

....

....

EVENING

....

....

....

....

....

....

Your Mindfulness Practices

Your mindfulness practices should feel fun—not like homework! They're meant to help you. Mindfulness is about exploring things and being curious. Like so many activities, such as playing a sport or musical instrument, the more you use your mindfulness practices, the better you will get at being mindful. And the more mindful you are, the easier it will be to bring awareness to different parts of your everyday life. Perhaps the most important thing to know about your mindfulness practices is that it is completely up to you to decide which practices you use and when you use them.

This book is here to help you learn to use mindfulness regularly. It might be helpful for you to think about your routine and when you might be able to fit in mindfulness practices each day. Can you spare some time in the morning or evening to try a practice? How about during your school day? Doing a mindfulness practice for just one to three minutes each day can make a huge difference. No start is too small. All that matters is that you get started!

As you continue to explore this book, you'll discover that mindfulness can help with lots of different experiences. These include feeling prepared for your day, focusing, understanding your feelings, managing your worries, staying calm, making good decisions, being kind, and winding down at the end of the day.

There's so much to explore—so let's move on!

CHAPTER 2

PREPARE FOR THE DAY AHEAD

Mindfulness can help you start off your day on the right foot feeling grounded and calm and looking forward to new experiences. Sometimes when you're having a tough week or you just need an energy boost, it helps to remember the power of a new day. Every day is a chance for a fresh start. Taking just a few minutes in the morning to do a mindfulness practice can help you feel relaxed. In this chapter, you'll explore different practices that can help you reset, feel prepared, and be ready to try new activities with an open mind and open heart.

Feeling Confident about Your Day

It was the last day of summer, and Nadia was feeling both scared and excited about her first day at her new school. In her mind she was thinking about all of the things that could go wrong. She kept asking herself, **"What if I don't make friends?"** *and* **"What if I don't like my teacher?"** *These thoughts took up a lot of space in her head and distracted her from fun activities. Her body was shaky, and she felt like she had butterflies in her stomach all day long. When it was time to go to bed, she struggled to fall asleep due to her racing thoughts and busy body.*

On the morning of the first day of school, Nadia jumped out of bed. She noticed that her heart was beating fast, so she paused and sat down on her bed. She took three deep breaths and was able to slow her breathing down. Because she brought her attention to what was happening in her body, she was also able to notice her thoughts. Nadia decided to open her journal. She wrote down five things she could do to calm down. She used this mindfulness practice to remind herself that no matter what happens in her day, she always has control over how she takes care of herself.

After taking a mindful moment to check in with herself, breathe, and reflect, Nadia was feeling more grounded than she had all week. She was still feeling a little scared and excited for her first day of school. But she felt less overwhelmed by her emotions and ready for this new experience.

Mindfulness can help you feel calm and confident for the day ahead. Whether you're going to school, playing sports, or meeting someone new, it is always helpful to take a moment to check in with yourself. You can ask yourself, *"How am I doing right now? What do I notice?"* Many mindfulness practices help you stay grounded and centered while you also stay connected to the present moment and what you are experiencing.

FEELINGS CHECK-IN

How are you feeling today? Circle all of the words that describe how you're feeling at this moment.

Sad

Happy

Jealous

Angry

Worried

Proud

Anxious

Calm

Frustrated

Irritable

Hopeful

Lonely

Overwhelmed

Curious

Playful

Tired

WHAT ARE YOUR INTENTIONS?

Take a moment to reflect on your goals, hopes, and dreams for the future.
Record them below.

Today, I hope that

....

....

In one year, I hope that

....

....

In five years, I hope that

....

....

Now close your eyes. What colors, sensations, and feelings come
to your mind when you think about your future self achieving
these goals, hopes, and dreams? Draw what you see.

CURIOSITY INVENTORY

Being mindful means being curious about what's happening around you. Curiosity helps you welcome new experiences and accept them as they are. What exactly does it mean to be curious? Curiosity means wondering about things and wanting to learn more about them. It inspires us to learn from people and situations. Human beings are always changing, and curiosity helps us stay aware of all the ways we're growing.

> Take a moment to reflect: What are some things about the world you're curious about? What are some things about other people you're curious about? What are some things about yourself you're curious about? Write down all your curiosities below.

THE WORLD:

....

....

....

....

OTHERS:

....

....

....

....

MYSELF:

....

....

....

....

KEEPING CONFIDENT

When you set goals for yourself and remember what you're proud of, it helps you feel confident throughout the day. Another way to stay confident is to take care of yourself. You can do this by making time for activities that make you feel balanced and happy, such as talking to a friend, creating art, or playing a game.

Think about the different ways that you can take care of your body and mind today.

THREE GOALS I HAVE FOR MYSELF ARE:

....

....

....

SOMETHING I'M PROUD OF MYSELF FOR IS:

....

....

....

AN ACTIVITY THAT MAKES ME FEEL GOOD IS:

....

....

....

I'LL TAKE CARE OF MY BODY TODAY BY:

....

....

....

WAKE UP, BODY!

This mindfulness practice uses breathing and movement to help you wake up your body. It also lets you check in with how you're feeling before you start your day. You might try this practice right after waking up or before leaving your house for school.

First, take a moment to check in with yourself. How are you feeling at this moment?

....

....

....

....

....

Settle into a chair or a sitting position on the floor. Try keeping your eyes open for this practice. Gaze at a spot on the floor in front of you. Keep your gaze steady. Now, start gently waking up your body. Slowly rotate your neck to one side and then the other side. Do this three times. Next, bring both shoulders up to your ears and roll them down toward your back. Then, rotate one shoulder in a circle three times. Rotate the other shoulder three times. Now, make your back really straight and bring your attention to your breath. Take three deep breaths, inhaling through the nose and exhaling through the mouth. Every time you inhale, sweep your arms up above your head so your hands touch. Pretend you're painting a sunrise in the air around you. As you exhale, bring your arms slowly back down to your sides. Do this three times. Notice how your body feels.

Take a moment to check in with yourself again. How do you feel after doing this practice?

....

....

....

....

I'M GRATEFUL FOR . . .

Taking a moment to remember what you are grateful for can help you stay grounded and make you feel happy. Reflect on what you're grateful for and record your thoughts below.

A person I am grateful for:

....

....

....

....

....

A memory I am grateful for:

....

....

....

....

....

An accomplishment of mine I am grateful for:

....

....

....

....

....

A place I am grateful for:

....

....

....

....

....

A hard experience I am grateful for:

....

....

....

....

....

A strength of mine I am grateful for:

....

....

....

....

....

MESSAGE TO MYSELF

An *affirmation* is a positive message that you can say to yourself whenever you need a boost. Read the affirmations below. Circle the one you plan to use today.

"I AM LOVED VERY MUCH."

"I WILL HAVE A GOOD DAY."

"I CAN LEARN FROM MYSELF AND OTHERS."

"I WILL BE KIND TO MYSELF AND OTHERS."

"I AM READY FOR WHATEVER COMES."

Come up with some affirmations of your own and write them here.

....

....

....

....

....

CHAPTER 3

FIND YOUR FOCUS

Have you ever been called on in class and didn't know what to say because you were thinking about something else? Or were you ever talking to a friend about something and then got distracted by something else and forgot what you were talking about?

This chapter will teach you how mindfulness can help you stay focused at school, at home, and when you're with your friends. Finding your focus makes learning in class easier and helps strengthen your relationships. It can also help when you're involved with your different hobbies, like sports, music, and art. Over the next few pages, you'll explore some fun mindfulness practices that will help you build your focusing muscles.

Where's Your Attention?

Kendrick invited his friend Riley to come over one afternoon. Kendrick and Riley played in the backyard for a while, then went inside to work on an art project together. They kept laughing at silly things and were having a great time together. After a few minutes of working on the art project, Kendrick remembered he had downloaded a new game on his tablet that he wanted to show Riley.

"Hold on a second," Kendrick said. "I want to show you something!" He left the room and came back with his tablet, already searching for the new game he had downloaded. "This game is so cool. You're going to love it!" he said to Riley with his eyes still locked on the screen.

"All right, cool," Riley said, smiling eagerly. He watched as Kendrick scrolled through different screens. Kendrick finally found the game and opened it, then started playing while Riley watched. After a few minutes of watching Kendrick play the game on his tablet, Riley wasn't smiling anymore. He was starting to feel bored.

"Hey, Kendrick, can we do something else?" Riley asked.

Kendrick continued playing and didn't respond, as if he hadn't heard Riley.

"Kendrick!" Riley said a little louder.

"Oh, sorry. What did you just say?" Kendrick said as he looked up at Riley.

"Can we do something else?" Riley said. "This is boring."

"Yeah, sure. I was having more fun before anyway," said Kendrick as he put aside the tablet. "This thing is so distracting."

Oftentimes there are many things going on around us—and in our heads—that can distract us. This makes staying focused and concentrating really hard! Like other skills, paying attention takes practice. Mindfulness helps you stay focused because it guides you as you bring your attention back to one thing at a time. It helps you notice when your mind drifts off or wanders to something else. The more you practice noticing when your mind wanders and bringing it back to what you want to focus on, the easier it is to do.

FEELING FOCUSED

Take a moment to think about how your body and mind feel when you're distracted. When some people feel distracted, they find it hard to keep still. Sometimes they have *racing thoughts*. Racing thoughts are thoughts that go through the mind really fast and change quickly. How do you know when you're feeling distracted?

I know I'm feeling distracted when my mind is

....

....

I know I'm feeling distracted when my body feels

....

....

Now take a moment to reflect on how your body and mind feel when you're feeling focused. When some people feel focused, they are able to stay on task and have a calm body. How do you know when you're feeling focused?

I know I'm feeling focused when my mind is

....

....

I know I'm feeling focused when my body feels

....

....

Our minds and bodies give us signals about when we're distracted and when we're focused. Paying attention to those signals can help us understand when we need to use a mindfulness practice to bring back our focus.

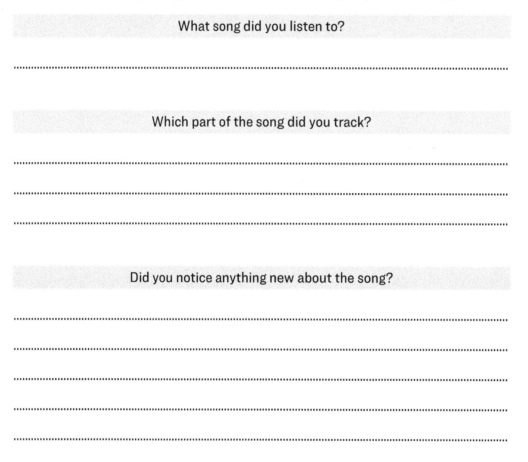

TRACKING A TUNE

This exercise gives you a chance to practice being mindful using music. Choose a song you enjoy listening to. Try listening to the song mindfully by choosing one part of the song to pay attention to. This could be the vocals, the beat, or the melody. Try tracking that part of the song from the beginning to the end. If your mind wanders during the song, bring your attention back to the part you're tracking.

What song did you listen to?

....

Which part of the song did you track?

....

....

....

Did you notice anything new about the song?

....

....

....

....

....

....

Mindful listening is a helpful skill that we can use when we're having a conversation with our family and friends. It can help us be "active listeners"—which means we listen carefully to others when they are talking so they feel heard and understood. When we listen actively, we can respond thoughtfully.

MIRROR, MIRROR

This activity strengthens your ability to focus on objects you see in front of you. This can help you pay better attention and stay focused when learning at school, playing sports, or making art. Sit or stand in front of a large mirror. Bring your hands up and hold them out in front of you so you can see their reflection in the mirror. Set your attention on the reflection of your hands. Now slowly move your hands in whatever way you want—but keep your attention on the reflection of your hands in the mirror. When your eyes or mind wander somewhere else, gently bring them back to the reflection of your hands. Next, bring your attention to your real hands. Start by taking a few moments to notice your left hand. Then notice your right hand. Again, if your eyes or mind wander, gently bring your attention back to your hands. After a few moments, drop your hands back down to your sides. Check in with your mind and body. How are you feeling?

Was this activity easy or hard? Were you able to notice when your mind or eyes wandered away from the reflection of your hands? Record your thoughts about your experience.

....

....

....

....

....

....

....

....

....

A SENSATIONAL WALK

If your body is having a hard time settling down, try going for a mindful walk! This activity allows you to move your body while you practice bringing your focus to three different senses: touch, sight, and hearing. You can do this walk outside or down a hallway at your school. Start by noticing the sensation of your feet on the ground. How do your feet feel as you walk? Next, bring your attention to what you see around you. Take a few moments to notice the different objects you see on your walk. Try noticing objects that are large and objects that are very small. Can you locate objects that are moving and objects that are still? Finally, bring your attention to what you hear. Take a few more moments to notice the sounds you hear on your walk. Try listening to sounds that are far away and sounds that are very close to you. Perhaps you can hear sounds that are quiet and sounds that are loud. When you're ready, bring your attention back to the sensation of your feet on the ground.

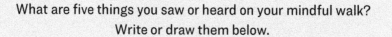

**What are five things you saw or heard on your mindful walk?
Write or draw them below.**

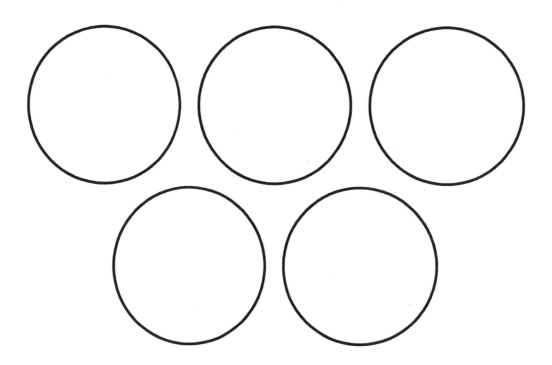

Tip: A mindful walk is a great way to find your focus when it's hard to sit still or pay attention at any given moment, whether at school or at home.

DOODLING THE DETAILS

This activity reminds you that being able to stay focused for long periods of time improves with practice! The more you practice staying focused, the easier it becomes to pay attention. Choose an object inside your home. This could be a plant, a picture, or a piece of furniture. Find a comfortable seat near the object—about two or three feet away if it's small, four or five feet away if it's large. Start by scanning the object with your eyes. Notice the object as a whole, then bring your attention to the small details of the object. In the space below, draw the object with as much detail as you can—without removing your pencil or pen from the paper. Keep your eyes on the object, trying to find all of the details to include in your drawing. When you feel like you've noticed and drawn every detail of the object, stop and look at the drawing you've created! It's okay if the drawing doesn't look very accurate. As you keep practicing this activity and your focus improves, you may notice that your drawing becomes more and more detailed each time!

MOUNTAIN BREATHING

This balanced breathing practice calms your body and helps you find your focus. Close your eyes and imagine a large mountain in front of you. Imagine yourself walking up the mountain as you breathe in through your nose, then walking down the mountain as you breathe out through your mouth. Try holding your breath to slow down your breathing as you walk back to the starting point of your climb.

1. INHALE THROUGH YOUR NOSE FOR FOUR COUNTS.

2. EXHALE THROUGH YOUR MOUTH FOR FOUR COUNTS.

3. HOLD YOUR BREATH FOR FOUR COUNTS.

4. REPEAT THREE TIMES.

By finding balance through your breath, you can help your body stay calm and focused when you need it to be, like when you're working on a big project at school or doing your homework.

GLITTER GAZING

Everyone experiences a busy mind at different times throughout the day. By imagining your busy mind calming down, you will be better able to tune in to the present moment and keep your focus as you move through your day! Find a comfortable seat either on the floor or in a chair. Try closing your eyes for this practice. Begin by imagining a jar filled with water, with a layer of glitter resting on the bottom. Now imagine giving the jar a good shake. See the glitter scatter all through the water, moving quickly in different directions. This might remind you of your mind when it's busy—with many thoughts going in all directions! Take in a breath. As you exhale, imagine the glitter slowing down a little. As you keep breathing, inhaling and exhaling, imagine the glitter gently falling to the bottom of the jar. Once all of the glitter has settled at the bottom, imagine looking through the water. It's clearer now, isn't it? Slowly open your eyes. Notice if anything has shifted or changed. How do your body and mind feel?

Draw what the mind jar looked like in the space below.

CHAPTER 4

GET TO KNOW YOUR FEELINGS

One of the most powerful things we can be mindful of is our own emotions. Everyone experiences a bunch of different emotions every day. Everyone's experience with feelings is different! No matter what your experience is, mindfulness can help you gain awareness of your emotions. It also helps you learn to respond in a thoughtful way to different feelings rather than to react thoughtlessly. This chapter will help you get in touch with your feelings and discover different mindfulness practices that you can use to manage tough feelings when they come along.

Feel Your Feelings

> *Kai was having a tough day. He was feeling sad, like a rain cloud was following him all day long. His body was tired and heavy. Every time his eyes filled up with tears, he tried to push the sadness away. That only seemed to make things worse and the rain cloud grow bigger!*
>
> *On his walk home from school, he felt his eyes fill up with tears again. This time, instead of trying to stop himself from crying, he let his tears flow. More and more tears came. After just a few moments of crying, he felt relieved and his body felt lighter. His sadness didn't feel so heavy anymore, and the rain cloud disappeared. Kai took one big breath and let it all go.*

Have you ever watched clouds drift by in the sky? You might have noticed that clouds come in all shapes and sizes. Some clouds are light and airy, and others are dark and heavy. In a lot of ways, feelings are like clouds. Some feelings lift us up, and other feelings weigh us down. And like clouds, feelings come and go—they shift and change.

We all experience many different feelings every day. Some feel good, and some feel bad. There are times when you might be able to identify a trigger, or a cause, for why you have a certain feeling. Other times, you might not know why you're feeling the way you do.

Feelings like anger, sadness, frustration, and anxiety can cause us to react or behave in ways that don't actually help us feel better. On top of that, we sometimes judge ourselves for having these feelings. That definitely doesn't help either!

Even though we can't control the feelings we experience at any particular moment, we *can* decide how we're going to respond to our feelings as they come up. That's where mindfulness comes in! Using mindfulness can help you have more control over how you respond to your feelings.

Being mindful of your feelings means being aware of your feelings. Everyone experiences feelings differently. For example, some people might get quiet when they are feeling sad, while other people might cry. It's important that you get to know your own experience with different feelings. By becoming more aware of your feelings, you will be less likely to judge them. Then you can learn to accept them as they are.

Learning how to *respond* to feelings instead of *reacting* to them will also help you make better decisions. Most of the time, reacting to feelings doesn't actually help us feel better. A feeling of anger might make you want to yell at someone or throw something. But by getting better at noticing when you're feeling angry, you might be able to take some deep breaths and talk to someone as a way to deal with the anger.

When you're mindful of your feelings, you have more control over how you respond to them—and more control over what you can do to take care of yourself!

WHY I FEEL...

Sometimes we experience a feeling because of something that happened. To better understand our emotions, it can be helpful to identify the different triggers, or causes, for different emotions. That way, we can be better prepared to respond to these feelings when they arise. Take a moment to reflect on and identify the different people, places, and things that trigger different feelings for you.

Something that makes me feel happy is

....

....

....

....

Something that makes me feel sad is

....

....

....

....

Something that makes me feel angry is

....

....

....

....

Something that makes me feel proud is

....

....

....

....

Something that makes me feel jealous is

....

....

....

....

Something that makes me feel anxious is

....

....

....

....

Something that makes me feel calm is

....

....

....

....

FACING YOUR FEELINGS

One of the ways we can tell how someone is feeling is by paying attention to their facial expressions. In the same way, other people try to figure out how we're feeling by noticing our facial expressions.

Think about four different emotions you have experienced recently. How do you look when you have those feelings? Are your face muscles relaxed or are they tense? Are you smiling or frowning? In the boxes below, draw your face when you experience those different feelings. Write the name of each feeling under its picture.

WHAT COLOR ARE YOU FEELING TODAY?

Take a moment to check in with your mind and body. What emotions are coming up right now? You might notice one feeling or many different feelings. Try naming the different emotions you notice, without judging them. Write down the names of the feelings you notice in the balloons below. Now think about each of those feelings, one at a time. What color comes to your mind when you think about each feeling? Is the feeling bright or pale? Dark or light? Warm or cool? If you're having trouble, close your eyes, say the feeling word out loud, and notice what color comes into your mind. Now color in the balloons, matching each feeling with its color.

EMOTION EXPLORER

Sometimes when we experience a difficult feeling like anger, sadness, or anxiety, we try to push the feeling away. In a lot of ways, this reaction makes sense. Some feelings don't feel good, but that's okay. The important thing to realize is this: Trying to avoid or push away tough feelings doesn't actually make them go away. This reaction actually makes those feelings more powerful.

Instead of trying to push away or avoid a tough feeling, try responding to it by exploring it and asking questions. Use the steps below to guide your exploration. Begin by choosing an emotion.

The emotion I'm exploring is

....

1. Does the feeling feel good, bad, or neutral?

....

....

2. How is my body responding to the feeling? (Think about your facial expression, breathing, physical sensations, and body posture.)

....

....

3. What thoughts am I having in connection to the feeling?

....

....

By using these steps to explore your tough feelings, the feelings become less powerful and scary. You'll feel like you have more control and can handle tough feelings when they arise.

BELLY BREATHING

When you control your breathing, signals are sent to your brain and body to calm down. This is helpful when you're feeling frustrated, anxious, or sad. For this practice, you can choose to lie down or sit in a comfortable chair. To begin, place your hands on your belly. Notice your breath as it is. Feel your belly rise as you inhale and lower as you exhale. For the next three breaths, inhale slowly through your nose as you feel your belly inflate like a balloon. Try to get your belly as big you can! Exhale slowly through your mouth as you feel your belly deflate. Breathing deeply from your belly helps you feel your breath in your body while also relaxing your body. When you're ready, gently open your eyes.

EMOTION CHARGER

Emotions are often connected to how much energy you have. If you have a lot of energy, your body might feel really frantic and busy. If you have little or no energy, your body might feel slow and sluggish. If your energy level is right in the middle, your body might feel calm and focused.

Read through the emotion words in the word bank, then sort them by their energy level. Write each emotion in one of the energy boxes.

Content   Anxious   Lonely   Sad
Overwhelmed   Disappointed
Hopeful   Worried   Proud
Interested   Excited   Frustrated
Bored   Confident   Tired   Angry

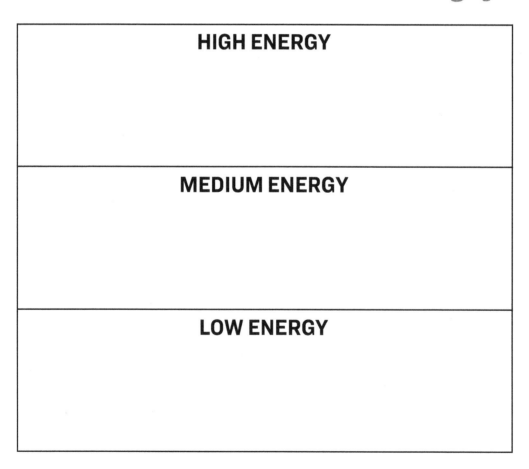

HIGH ENERGY

MEDIUM ENERGY

LOW ENERGY

FEELING CLOUDS

Remember how we compared feelings to clouds earlier? Like clouds drifting across the sky, feelings come and go. The following meditation helps you explore what it feels like to allow different feelings to just be what they are when they show up, while at the same time knowing that these feelings will pass. For this meditation, you can choose to lie down or sit in a comfortable chair. Close your eyes. Start by imagining that your different feelings are clouds in the sky. Imagine looking up at the sky and watching the feeling clouds drift by as you identify them. Don't try to change the feeling clouds as they pass by. Just observe them as they move across the sky. Notice the sizes of the different feeling clouds. Which feelings are big clouds? Which feelings are small clouds? Perhaps some of the clouds are light and airy, while others are dark and heavy. The shapes of the clouds might also be different. Try to notice how your body responds to the different feeling clouds as they pass by. Continue to watch the feeling clouds pass by, letting them come and go just as they are.

What feelings did you notice? Write them in the clouds below.

CHAPTER 5

WORK WITH YOUR WORRIES

Feeling worried is a lot like walking through mud. Imagine that with each step you take, your foot gets stuck. You notice that it's really hard to get your foot unstuck, which makes you worry that your foot is going to stay stuck! Mindfulness can help you find a way to stay calm when you find yourself moving through mud. By staying calm, you'll eventually find a way to get out of the mud and step onto some soft grass. In this chapter, you will learn how to cope with your worries when you find yourself getting stuck!

Everyone Has Worries

Kamal gets really nervous when he has to talk in front of the class because he worries that he will make mistakes. On Monday, his teacher assigned everyone in the class a five-minute presentation to give on Friday. When his teacher made the announcement, Kamal noticed that his hands started shaking, his heart was beating quickly, and his stomach started hurting.

*The next few nights, Kamal had trouble falling asleep because he was worried about his presentation. He kept thinking, **"What if I mess up?"** and **"What if someone laughs at me?"** He tried pushing the thoughts away and thinking about something else, but the thoughts kept coming back.*

On Friday morning, Kamal woke up feeling very anxious and worried. He took a moment to sit down and try to calm his nerves. For the first time all week, he admitted to himself that he was feeling anxious and worried, and he identified his feelings. Just doing that made him feel calmer.

*Next, he tried a relaxation breathing practice to slow down his breathing. This helped his body feel less shaky. When the **"What if?"** thoughts came into his head, he gently said to himself, **"I'm worrying right now."** By taking a moment to notice how he was doing and naming his feelings, he gave himself a tool to calm down. This made him feel like he had more control over his mind and body than his anxiety did.*

Most people experience some stress, worry, and anxiety every day in both their mind and their body. You might get the same thoughts over and over again, like they're on a loop. Your breathing might speed up, or you might have trouble breathing at all. Anxiety can make your face feel hot, your heart beat fast, your legs feel shaky, and your stomach ache.

Sometimes we feel worried about things we don't have any control over. Anxiety might make you feel like you don't have any control over the thoughts in your mind or how your body acts. Mindfulness can help you manage your worries. It reminds you that you always have control over how you respond to anxiety. Mindfulness exercises like breathing, movement, and meditation can also help your body calm down.

Mindfulness is a tool that can be used along with exercise, eating healthy foods, and talk therapy to help manage anxiety and worry. If your anxiety or worry prevents you from enjoying activities you usually love or interferes with everyday activities like going to school, you should talk to a trusted adult about exploring some other ways you can get support.

STRESS STARTERS

Below are some situations and activities that can cause stress and anxiety. Which ones make you feel anxious? Circle them.

CONFLICT OR DRAMA IN MY FAMILY

CONFLICT OR DRAMA WITH MY FRIENDS

HOMEWORK

MEETING NEW PEOPLE

ANSWERING QUESTIONS IN CLASS

PRESENTING IN FRONT OF THE CLASS

MAKING NEW FRIENDS

SUDDEN CHANGES IN MY ROUTINE OR SCHEDULE

GETTING MY GRADES

SCHOOLWORK

FEELING LEFT OUT OF MY FRIEND CIRCLE

WORRIES IN YOUR BODY

Being aware of how your body acts when you're feeling worried can help you know when to use a tool to calm down. Sometimes when people feel worried, their legs feel shaky, their belly feels sick, and their chest feels tight. Take a moment to think about how your body acts when you feel worried.

I know I'm feeling worried or anxious when my body

....

....

....

....

....

What physical sensations do you feel in your legs, belly, and chest when you're worried? Draw a picture of how your body looks when you're feeling worried or anxious.

BLOWING WORRY BUBBLES

This exercise involves two mindfulness practices: relaxation breathing, which helps send signals to the body to calm down, and a visualization, which can help calm the mind. (A *visualization* is a picture you make in your mind.) Settle into a sitting position either on the floor or in a chair. Close your eyes. Take a moment to think about any worries you may have. Now raise one hand out in front of you and imagine that you're holding a bubble wand. Put your other hand on your belly. Inhale through your nose, feeling your belly rise. Exhale through your mouth, breathing out slowly as though you're blowing bubbles through your wand. After you exhale, imagine that all of the bubbles you've just blown are filled with your worries, and they are now floating around you. Imagine all of the bubbles floating away from you as you keep breathing in through your nose and out through your mouth. After five deep breaths, gently open your eyes.

In the bubbles below, draw or write down the worries that you watched float away.

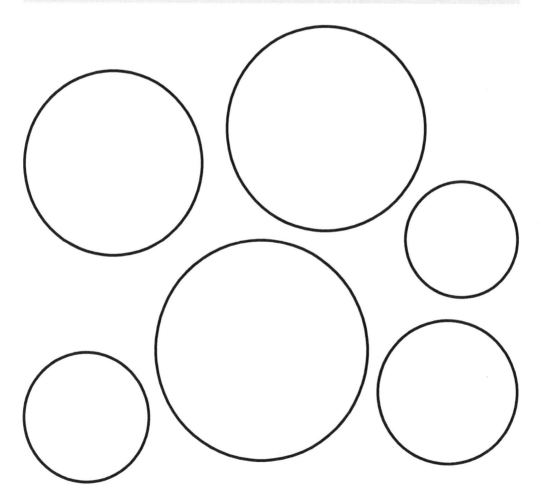

WASH AWAY YOUR WORRIES

This practice helps you calm your body by directing your attention to your sense of touch. Wash your hands under cold running water. Focus your attention on how the cold water feels on your hands. If your mind wanders to something else, gently bring it back to the feeling of the water on your hands. Let the sensation of the water on your hands wash away whatever worry thoughts and feelings you have in your mind and body.

SQUEEZE AND RELEASE

Find a seat either on the floor or in a chair. You can also choose to lie down on your back. Close your eyes.

For this practice, you are going to do a body scan. You are going to try to squeeze and tense up different parts of your body and then release them. Start by bringing your attention to your toes and feet. Squeeze your feet and toes for three seconds. Release the squeeze, letting go of the tension. Notice how it feels to let go of any tightness in your feet.

Next, squeeze your legs for three seconds, then release. Continue to move up your body, squeezing your hands, arms, and shoulders for three seconds and then releasing. When you get to your head, squeeze your face as though you just ate something really sour, then release. Finally, squeeze your entire body—then let it all go.

How did your body feel before the squeeze and release practice?

....

....

....

....

....

How did your body feel after the squeeze and release practice?

....

....

....

....

....

SKETCH A SONG

This practice connects music and drawing to help calm the mind and body.

For this activity, choose a song you enjoy listening to that makes you feel relaxed. As you listen to the song, draw whatever images come into your mind in the space below. Use whatever shapes, colors, and designs you would like to represent the song. Allow the music to help you create a calming picture.

NAMING YOUR NERVOUSNESS

Sometimes when we feel nervous or anxious, we have anxious thoughts. Anxious thoughts are thoughts that make you feel stressed, scared, and confused—and they keep coming back. It can be helpful to give a name to your nervousness or anxiety so you can identify it when you are feeling it. For example, say you name your nervousness Nicky. The next time you notice your heart is beating fast and you're having anxious thoughts, you can say to yourself, "I guess Nicky is here!" This helps you become aware of your feelings and reminds you that you have more control of your mind and body than the feelings do.

Create your nervousness character below.

1. The name of my nervousness or anxiety is

2. Draw a picture of what your nervousness or anxiety looks like.

3. How would you describe the voice of your nervousness? Is it loud and scary, or soft like a whisper?

....

....

....

CHAPTER 6

STAY CALM IN TOUGH SITUATIONS

Mindfulness can help you stay calm and relaxed when you're dealing with tough situations at school, at home, or with your friends. Tricky situations can make you feel overwhelmed with different feelings. Sometimes, these big feelings can get in the way of other positive experiences, activities, and thoughts. Remembering to stay mindful will help you handle these emotions throughout the day, no matter what challenges you face! In this chapter, you will learn some ways to handle challenging situations so you will feel prepared and confident when these situations happen.

Keeping Your Cool

Yuki was playing soccer with two of her friends after school. She was having fun playing with her friends until one of them told her she wasn't very good at passing the ball and said she should watch so she could learn how to play.

As Yuki sat at the edge of the field and watched her two friends play together, she started feeling bored. When she asked her friends if she could join the game again, they laughed and ignored her.

This made Yuki feel really hurt. Her eyes started filling with tears and she was clenching her fists tightly. She noticed that her body felt shaky. She suddenly felt like she wanted to yell at her friends to tell them how mean they were and then run away.

When Yuki noticed her hurt feelings, she knew she had to do something to take care of herself. She closed her eyes and thought of her backyard at home. It was her happy place and made her feel calm. After a few moments, she opened her eyes and noticed she felt a little better.

She stood up and walked over to her friends. She told them how she was feeling and said, "It hurt me when you ignored me and laughed. Can we all play together now?"

Her friends stopped playing and looked at her. They both apologized and said they realized that what they did was mean. Yuki smiled, and they all started playing together again.

Challenging things happen almost every day. Close your eyes for a moment and think about the challenges, big and small, that you might come across during your day. You might consider challenges that could happen at home or at school. Perhaps you're thinking about a difficult school assignment, or a sudden change in your schedule, or a conflict with your friends. What *feelings* came up for you as you thought about these challenges? Maybe you noticed feeling frustrated, over-whelmed, or hurt.

Even though we can't always control what obstacles we come across, we do get to decide how to respond to them. This is much easier to do when you use mindfulness practices regularly! Mindfulness can help you stay calm under pressure and manage strong emotions as they happen. When you admit that you're dealing with a difficult situation and you become aware of your feelings, you'll be better able to keep your cool, solve the problem, and move forward with your day.

Sometimes you may need help to stay calm when you're taking a big test, playing a competitive game, or having an argument with a family member or a friend. By doing mindfulness practices and checking in with your feelings, you'll be able to focus on the present moment and find a way to take care of your feelings. In challenging moments, self-reflection, controlled breathing, and moving your body are all helpful strategies! By managing your feelings when a challenge comes up, you'll find a way to handle the situation thoughtfully and discover how you can learn from it.

WHERE IN MY BODY?

Becoming aware of how your body responds when different feelings happen can help you know how to respond to these feelings in a calm way.

Take a moment to think about how your body responds when you're dealing with a tough situation and feeling strong emotions.
Where do you experience these emotions in your body?

My _____ feels _____ when I'm angry.

My _____ feels _____ when I'm frustrated.

My _____ feels _____ when I'm hurt.

My _____ feels _____ when I'm overwhelmed.

My _____ feels _____ when I'm under pressure.

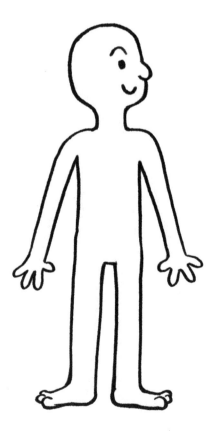

SHAKE IT UP!

Sometimes when people have strong emotions, their bodies get a rush of energy. One way to burn off this energy is by moving the body. Stand in an area where you have some room to move. Start by shaking one arm, then shake the other arm. Shake one leg, then shake the other leg. Finally, for a minute or two, let go and shake your whole body! Stop shaking. Put one hand on your heart and one hand on your belly. Notice how your body feels now that you've moved it.

In the space below, draw a picture of how your body feels after shaking it up.

SPIN THE WHEEL!

Note: Feel free to use a pinwheel for this practice if you have one at home. If not, use your imagination! Find a seat either on the floor or in a chair. Close your eyes for this practice. Imagine that you're holding a pinwheel out in front of you with one hand. Put your other hand on your belly. When you imagine your pinwheel, decide what color you want it to be. Try choosing a color that gives you a feeling of calm. The goal of this activity is to have the pinwheel spin for as long as possible. To do this, you're going to breathe out through your mouth slowly. Start by taking a deep breath, inhaling through your nose. Feel your belly rise. Exhale through your mouth, breathing out as slowly as you can. Imagine the pinwheel starting to spin. Inhale and exhale again, and then again. Imagine the pinwheel spinning more and more each time you exhale. After three deep breaths, gently open your eyes.

How do you feel after doing pinwheel breathing?

....

....

....

....

MY HAPPY PLACE

Find a seat either on the floor or in a chair. Close your eyes for this practice. Think of a place where you've spent some time that gave you a feeling of peace and joy. It might be a place that is familiar to you and brings you comfort, like a room in your house. Or it could be a place you've visited, like a park or a beach. As you think about this happy place, try to use your senses to create a full picture. What would you see if you were there? What would you hear? What would you smell? Let yourself just be in this happy place for a few moments. How does it feel to be there? When you're ready, gently open your eyes. Record your experience.

When I think of my happy place:

I see

....

....

....

....

I hear

....

....

....

....

I smell

....

....

....

....

I feel

....

....

....

....

Draw a picture of your happy place below.

TURNING NEGATIVES INTO POSITIVES

We all experience negative thoughts. Negative thoughts can make us feel anxious or upset, and they make it hard to see a situation the way it really is. This exercise will help you become more aware of the types of negative thoughts you have.

Read each statement below and its example. Put a check mark next to it if it describes a type of negative thought you sometimes have. Then write down your own negative thought.

❑ **I focus on the negative and forget the positive.**

Example: *"It doesn't matter that I participate a lot in class, because I failed the test."*

My negative thought:

❑ **I jump to conclusions.**

Example: *"Maggie didn't say hi to me this morning, so she must be mad at me."*

My negative thought:

❑ **I blame myself or others.**

Example: *"I made a mistake during the game, and that's why my team lost."*

My negative thought:

❑ **I think in extreme terms.**

Example: *"I can't draw, so I'm a terrible artist."*

My negative thought:

....

❑ **I put labels on myself or others.**

Example: *"I got a C on my homework because I'm stupid."*

My negative thought:

....

How can you change your negative thoughts so that they are more positive and you can see the whole picture? Write a few positive thoughts below.

....

....

....

CALMING COLOR

Find a comfortable seat and close your eyes. Think about a color that you find calming. Next, bring your focus to your breath, inhaling through your nose and exhaling through your mouth. Imagine that each time you inhale, you breathe in your calming color, and your body relaxes. With each exhale, you breathe out your calming color, and your body releases all its stress. Take three deep breaths.

What calming color did you see?

LIFE LESSONS

When you take some time to think about the challenges you come across in your daily life, you'll find that you can learn from your experiences and grow as a person.

In the space below, journal about a difficult situation you faced. How did this experience make you feel? How did you respond to it? How did you grow from the experience?

CHAPTER 7

MAKE YOUR BEST
DECISION

CHAPTER 7

MAKE YOUR BEST DECISION

Have you ever been caught in a storm? If you've ever seen a thunderstorm begin really quickly, you might have noticed the wind starting to blow, dark clouds rolling by, and rain pouring down—and it all seems to happen in just a few minutes!

Sometimes our feelings take over our body just as fast as a thunderstorm happens. In those moments, we can get caught off guard and react to our feelings without thinking first. Mindfulness can help by reminding us to take a moment to think about our emotions and the challenges we're dealing with *before* we respond to them. When we do that, we're better able to make good decisions.

Mindful Actions

Nico was writing an essay for school on his computer. He was finally almost finished after two hours of working on it.

He stepped away from his computer and returned a few minutes later. He was shocked when he realized that the essay had accidentally been deleted from his computer. Suddenly, Nico started feeling really frustrated. His face became hot, and he felt like he was going to explode! When his dad came over and asked what was wrong, Nico buried his head in his hands and wanted to scream. Instead, he paused to name how he was feeling and said to himself, **"It's okay. I'm frustrated right now."** *This helped him feel more in control of his frustration instead of feeling like his frustration was taking over.*

Nico lifted his head and looked up at his dad. "My essay got deleted and now I'm feeling really frustrated," he said. His dad sat down with him and said, "That is super-frustrating. I'm sorry that happened. Let's figure out a way to move forward and get it done together." Nico felt relieved.

Staying mindful throughout your day can help you pause and think before you act, no matter what decisions you have to make.

Often when we feel angry, annoyed, or frustrated, we react quickly to these feelings and make choices that may not help us feel better. For example, if someone becomes really angry after a friend says something mean, they might react without thinking by pushing that friend. Or someone who is frustrated with their homework might yell and throw their pencil on the ground. In both of these situations, the reactions don't actually help the person feel better. In fact, their reactions might make their anger and frustration feel even more out of control!

Mindfulness helps you have more control over how you respond to your emotions, even when they happen quickly. By being mindful of your feelings in these moments, you'll be better able to respond to these feelings and situations in a thoughtful way. Mindfulness allows you to see the whole picture so that you don't get stuck in a feeling and react before taking a moment to reflect and breathe.

REACTING VS. RESPONDING

Reacting to feelings means responding quickly without giving much thought or awareness to your action. Reacting can sometimes lead you to make a choice that doesn't help you or others feel better. Some examples of reacting include yelling or hitting something.

What are some other examples of reacting to feelings?

....

....

....

....

....

....

Responding thoughtfully to feelings means staying calm and thinking before you act. Responding to feelings in a thoughtful way usually leads you to make a choice that helps you and others feels better. Some examples of responding thoughtfully include calmly expressing your feelings to someone or counting to 10 before you speak or act.

What are some other examples of responding thoughtfully to feelings?

....

....

....

....

....

....

....

STORM SIGNALS

This journaling practice can help you become more aware of the signals of an incoming emotional storm! The signals are sent by your mind and body to let you know that a strong emotion may be about to overwhelm you. The more aware you are of the signals you're getting, the better able you will be to respond to the emotion in a thoughtful way when it shows up. Can you remember a time when you reacted to your feelings without thinking? Maybe you were angry and said something hurtful that you didn't mean. Or maybe you were frustrated with your homework and slammed your books down.

Write about a time when you reacted without thinking.

....

....

....

....

What signals does your body give you that you are becoming angry, frustrated, or annoyed?

....

....

....

....

What signals does your mind give you that you are becoming angry, frustrated, or annoyed?

....

....

....

....

A GOOD SIGH!

This breathing practice can help you let go of anger or frustration so you can calm down. When you're calm, you can respond in a thoughtful way to tough feelings when they rise up.

Start by checking in with your feelings and your body. How are you feeling?

....

....

....

....

....

Settle into a seat either on the floor or in a chair. Close your eyes for this practice. Place one hand on your belly and one hand on your heart. Inhale through your nose and exhale through your mouth. When you exhale, try to let out a BIG SIGH. Make it loud if you want! Notice how it feels when you let your breath go in that big, loud sigh. When you let it go, imagine that you're also letting go of your anger or frustration. Take three more deep breaths, sighing each time you exhale. When you're ready, gently open your eyes.

Check in again with your feelings and your body. Do you feel any different now?

....

....

....

....

....

A HANDY PRACTICE

Bringing awareness to your body can help you let go of strong feelings like anger and frustration. When you release these feelings, you have more control in the moment to make good decisions. Start by clenching your hands into fists. Hold for three seconds. Unclench your hands. Notice how it feels to let your hands relax. Next, bring your attention to the different fingers on each hand. Bring your attention to your left pinkie, then your right pinkie. Left pointer finger, then right pointer finger. Left thumb, then right thumb. Continue to bring your attention to each finger.

Trace your hand in the space below. Keep your attention on the sensation of your pen or pencil tracing around your hand. Once you have a picture of your hand, color it in with a calming color.

WALK IT OFF

Sometimes the best thing to do when you feel a strong, difficult emotion is to give yourself some space to calm down. When you're calm, you're much more likely to respond to your emotion in a thoughtful way and make a good decision. This practice helps you get space while slowing down your body. Start by walking very quickly or running for 10 steps. Either count out loud or to yourself. When you have done 10 steps, put one hand on your heart and one hand on your belly. Notice how your body feels. Take another 10 steps, this time slowing down your pace to a medium speed. Again, after the 10 steps, put one hand on your heart and one hand on your belly. Notice how your body feels now. Finally, take 10 more steps, this time moving as slowly as you can. Continue to count as you take each step. Notice how your body feels after taking this slow walk. Are you feeling any calmer?

ANGER AFFIRMATIONS

Emotions can build like an avalanche thundering down a mountain. This usually happens when we try to push our feelings away or try to ignore them. When we learn to accept our feelings as they are, they don't feel quite so big and powerful. Below are some affirmations you can use to let yourself feel anger without allowing the anger to take over. (Remember, an affirmation is a positive message that you say to yourself.) Using affirmations helps us stay in control and make thoughtful decisions.

Circle the affirmations you will use the next time you feel angry.

IT'S OKAY THAT I FEEL ANGRY.

MY ANGER DOESN'T NEED TO TAKE OVER.

I CAN BREATHE THROUGH MY ANGER.

THIS ANGER WILL PASS.

Can you think of some other affirmations you can use the next time you're feeling angry? Write them here.

....

....

....

....

PICKING YOUR PATHWAY

Sometimes you have to make a decision or take an action in response to a situation. Before you choose your decision or action, it can be helpful to think about all the pathways, or options, you can pick from. What choice can you make to best take care of your feelings? Mindfulness helps you take a moment to see all the pathways that are available and pick the one that you think will help you the most.

In the space below, write down or draw all the pathways you can take when you get in a fight with a friend or a family member.

In the space below, write down or draw all the pathways you can take when you don't do well on an assignment or quiz.

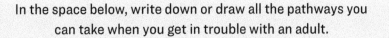

In the space below, write down or draw all the pathways you
can take when you get in trouble with an adult.

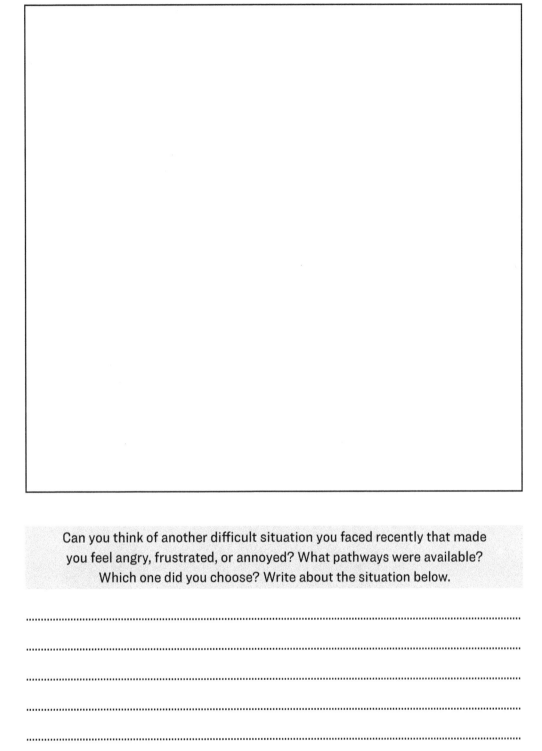

Can you think of another difficult situation you faced recently that made
you feel angry, frustrated, or annoyed? What pathways were available?
Which one did you choose? Write about the situation below.

....

....

....

....

....

CHAPTER 8

SHOW KINDNESS, COMPASSION, AND EMPATHY

Take a moment to think about a time when you felt someone's love for you or when you felt love for someone else. How did that make you feel? Perhaps you felt comforted, safe, and good about yourself. In a lot of ways, mindfulness can help you develop love and kindness toward both yourself and others. This chapter will give you tools and practices to help you develop empathy for others, while also allowing you to accept and feel compassion for yourself.

Be Kind to Yourself and Others

Roxanne was having a really bad day. During lunch, she noticed all of her friends sitting at a different table than usual. When she walked over and asked if she could join them, they told her there wasn't any more room. Roxanne ended up sitting by herself and felt alone and hurt.

After lunch, she kept trying to push away her hurt and sad feelings, but they kept coming back. She felt like something was wrong with her and that's why her friends didn't want her sitting with them.

When she got home from school, her mom asked how her day was. Roxanne responded by yelling, "I don't want to talk about it!" and ran up to her room. Roxanne's mom called after her. She was surprised and confused because she didn't know why Roxanne yelled at her.

When Roxanne got to her room, she started crying. She realized that her hurt and sad feelings from lunch had been with her all day. She took a moment to notice how she was feeling and think about why she was feeling that way. She realized she felt like she wasn't good enough, and that was making her sad.

Because she was now aware of her thoughts and feelings, Roxanne was able to take a deep breath and say to herself, "I am enough just as I am." Taking the time to be compassionate for her feelings made her feel better.

After a few minutes, Roxanne went back downstairs and said to her mom, "I'm sorry. I had a bad day and I wasn't taking care of my feelings. I didn't mean to take things out on you." Roxanne and her mom hugged, and Roxanne felt much better.

One of the most wonderful things about mindfulness is that it can help us be kind to others *and* to ourselves. Mindfulness involves learning to notice and accept your experiences without judging them. Mindfulness helps you welcome yourself with open and compassionate arms. By taking the time to notice your feelings and thoughts, you give yourself support and care.

Mindfulness can also help you be curious about other people's experiences. When you want to give support to others, it's helpful to have curiosity because it will encourage you to try to understand their experience. In other words, you will be curious about what their experience is like. And this is where empathy comes in!

Empathy means putting yourself in someone else's shoes, understanding their feelings, and sharing in their experience.

With compassion for yourself and empathy for others comes the power of gratitude, or feeling thankful. When you are grateful for your experiences, you accept that every experience, good and bad, helps you learn and grow. Gratitude also allows you to remember that it's important to take care of yourself and others each and every day!

HUGS ALL AROUND

Settle into a seat either on the floor or in a chair. Close your eyes. Bring your attention to your breath. Wrap your arms around your shoulders, as though you're giving yourself a hug. Notice how it feels to offer comfort and love to yourself. Next, inhale through your nose as you open your arms wide. Hold them out in front of you, as though you're hugging the air around you. Imagine that you are sending loving wishes to the world. Notice how it feels to be open and loving. As you exhale through your mouth, bring your arms back and give yourself a hug again. Take three more breaths, hugging yourself and hugging the world. Finally, put one hand on your heart and one hand on your belly. Notice how you feel now that you've sent love inward and outward.

SENDING KIND WISHES

Take a moment to find a comfortable position, either sitting or lying down. Close your eyes. Bring your attention to the sounds around you and the sensation of your body being supported by your chair or the floor (or whatever you're sitting or lying on). Notice how it feels to be with yourself in this moment. Begin by bringing to mind someone you care about deeply. Notice what feelings, sensations, and thoughts come up when you think about this person. Imagine sending kind wishes to this person, saying, "May you know joy, may you know peace, may you know you are worthy." Notice how it feels to send kind wishes to this person. Now bring to mind someone who makes you feel frustrated or annoyed. Notice what feelings, sensations, and thoughts come up when you think about this person. Again, imagine sending kind wishes to this person, saying, "May you know joy, may you know peace, may you know you are worthy." Notice how it feels to send kind wishes to this person. Finally, bring to mind a picture of yourself. Notice what feelings, sensations, and thoughts come up when you think about this picture of yourself. Again, imagine sending kind wishes to yourself, saying, "May you know joy, may you know peace, may you know you are worthy." Notice how it feels to send kind wishes to yourself.

How did it feel sending kind wishes to someone you care about deeply?

....

....

....

....

How did it feel sending kind wishes to someone who
makes you feel frustrated or annoyed?

....

....

....

....

How did it feel sending kind wishes to yourself?

....

....

....

....

....

....

A FULL HEART

What people, activities, and things do you love? Fill in the outline below with all the things that are in your heart. Feel free to use colors, drawings, and words.

LETTER TO A BEST FRIEND

Having compassion for yourself means treating yourself with the same respect and kindness you would have for a best friend. But you might notice that the way you talk to a best friend is a little different from the way you talk to yourself. Write a letter to yourself as though you were your own best friend. What would you tell yourself you're grateful for? What strengths would you focus on? What good qualities would you point out? What would you say you're proud of yourself for?

Dear Me,

....

....

....

....

....

....

....

....

....

....

Sincerely,

A HELPING HAND FOR THE HURT

To offer a helping hand to yourself, you need to name what hurts. Then you can ask yourself what you need from yourself to feel better.

If the hurting part of you could communicate, what would it express through words, feelings, and drawings? Draw or write down what your hurt wants to communicate.

What does the hurting part of you need to feel better? Does it need words of support or encouragement? Does it need you to breathe? Do you need to move your body? Draw or write down how you're going to take care of the hurting part of you below.

CALLING CARING WORDS

One of the most powerful ways we can be kind to ourselves when things are hard is to name our feelings and say some caring and compassionate words to ourselves. Complete the chart below with some kind words that can replace the harsh, judgmental words. Then come up with some examples of your own.

INSTEAD OF . . .	TRY . . .
"I'm not good enough."	"I am always enough."
"I'm a failure."	"My flaws make me human."
"Nobody understands me."	"Everyone struggles."
"I hate feeling this way."	
"Nobody cares about me."	

THANK-YOU NOTES

Telling people in your life that they're important can help make you and others feel joyful and loved. Use the space below to write thank-you notes to four different people in your life. You might tell them what you're grateful for, how they support you, and why they make you happy.

Hint: Take photos of each thank-you note, and send them to the people who are important to you!

....

....

....

....

....

....

....

CHAPTER 9

END YOUR DAY STRONG

It's the end of another day! At night, we sometimes feel restless, distracted, and stuck on everything that happened during the day. Have you ever felt that way? You can always turn to mindfulness to help you reflect and wind down before bed. Mindfulness can help relax the body and turn off busy thoughts so you can get to sleep and get the rest you need. This chapter will explore different practices that you can use to relax your body and calm your mind.

Sometimes You Just Have a Lot of Thoughts

> *Maya was having a hard time falling asleep. Her mind was busy with lots of different thoughts and worries that were keeping her awake. She kept trying to push the thoughts and worries away, but that only seemed to make them louder.*
>
> *Maya realized that pushing them away wasn't working. So she decided to try a body scan practice to bring her focus to how her body was feeling and calm down her thoughts. When she brought her awareness to her body, she noticed how tired her body was feeling. This helped her thoughts and worries quiet down. Her mind became calmer, and she was eventually able to fall asleep.*

Close your eyes and imagine yourself getting ready for bed. You woke up early today, had a busy day at school, participated in an activity after school, and spent some time in the evening doing homework. Now you are finally able to pause and be still. How is your body feeling? What emotions are you feeling? What thoughts are you having?

You might notice that you're feeling lots of mixed emotions about different events that happened throughout your day. Your body might be tired, but your mind might still be busy and swirling with thoughts. You might also be stuck thinking about a particular thing that happened during the day or what is going to come tomorrow. For all of these reasons, it's important to take some time at the end of the day to shift your attention back to the present moment and settle down before bed.

Mindfulness can help you relax and wind down at the end of your day. The evening is a great time to check in with your body, thoughts, and breathing. You can even create a regular mindfulness practice to do every evening. Try using one of the practices in this chapter before bed each night. Practicing mindfulness before bed will help you get a good night's sleep. The next few pages will introduce you to calming mindfulness practices that will help you end your day with a sense of gratitude and peace.

SOOTHING BREATH

Take a moment to check in with yourself. How are you feeling?

....

....

....

....

....

....

....

Settle into a seat, either on the floor or in a chair. Close your eyes or lower your gaze. For this practice, bring both hands to your heart. Call to mind an experience you had today that brought you joy or peace. Take a moment to feel gratitude for this experience. Inhale through your nose, saying to yourself, "I'm inhaling gratitude." Slowly exhale through your mouth, saying to yourself, "I'm exhaling relaxation." Take three more deep breaths, inhaling gratitude and exhaling relaxation.

Take a moment to check in with yourself again. How
do you feel now, after doing this practice?

....

....

....

....

....

....

....

MOON MANTRA

One way to help yourself wind down and relax at the end of the day is to use a mantra that you can focus on. (A *mantra* is a word or statement that is repeated over and over again during meditation.)

Circle the moon mantra below that you will use tonight.

BREATHE IN AND BREATHE OUT.

I AM CALM AND RELAXED.

MY MIND IS AT PEACE.

I AM LETTING GO OF MY DAY.

I AM LOOKING FORWARD TO TOMORROW.

Create a drawing to represent the moon mantra you chose. Use colors, shapes, and designs that are calming and relaxing.

TWIST AND STRETCH

You can calm your body before bed by gently stretching and moving into shapes and poses that help you feel relaxed. Start by lying on your back, on your bed or on the floor. Bring your knees into your chest. Give them a hug. Inhale through your nose as you hug your knees a little tighter. As you exhale, drop your knees to your right side while you turn your head to the left. Stay in this position for a moment or two. Next, bring your knees back into your chest, giving them a hug as you inhale through your nose. As you exhale, drop your knees to your left side while you turn your head to the right. Stay in this position for a moment or two. When you're ready, bring your knees back into your chest, inhaling through your nose. When you exhale, stretch out your legs and arms. Notice how it feels to be supported by the bed or floor beneath you.

STREAM OF THOUGHTS

This visualization practice can help calm your mind and thoughts before bed. (Remember, a visualization is a picture you make in your mind.) Find a comfortable position lying on your back. Close your eyes. Take a moment to notice any thoughts that are popping into your mind. Are you thinking about things in the past or in the future? Are you worrying about something that might happen? Notice how it feels to be having these thoughts. Now imagine that you're sitting next to a stream of gently flowing water. Notice what sounds you might hear sitting at the edge of this stream and what you might see. Take a moment to notice how it feels to be sitting by this softly flowing stream. Next, imagine that your thoughts are also flowing down the stream. Every time a thought pops into your mind, place it in the water and watch it float down the stream. Notice how it feels to watch your thoughts flow away. Perhaps you'll begin to realize that there are fewer and fewer thoughts floating down the stream. You might even get to a moment when you don't see any thoughts in the stream at all! The stream is only flowing water again, and your mind is clear and calm.

What thoughts did you place in the stream? Draw a picture of your stream of thoughts below.

MOONLIGHT BODY SCAN

This body scan practice helps your body release stress and get ready for sleep. Find a comfortable position lying down. Close your eyes. Imagine that you see the moon glowing above you. Take a moment to picture the glowing color. Perhaps the glow is a soft white, or a light blue, or a warm yellow. Choose a color that feels calming and relaxing to you. Now, as you inhale, imagine the glowing color of the moon moving slowly up your body, starting at your toes and feet. As the moon glow moves up your body, each body part becomes heavy and relaxed. Continue to inhale and exhale. Notice the moon glow move up your legs and through your belly, hands, arms, and shoulders. Let your body release any tension as the moon glow continues to move up with each breath, all the way to the top of your head. When you're ready, gently open your eyes.

Draw the moon you pictured in the space below.

How does your body feel after doing the moonlight body scan?

....

....

....

....

EMOTION MEDITATION

This meditation practice helps you reflect on emotions you felt during the day. Find a comfortable seat and close your eyes. Think about a feeling that was challenging for you today. Perhaps you've been feeling anxious, frustrated, sad, or scared. Notice any sensations that come up in your body when you remind yourself about this challenging feeling. Now imagine that each time you inhale, you are making space to hold this feeling. Imagine that each time you exhale, you are offering compassion to this feeling and to yourself. Take a moment to make space for this feeling. Inhale acceptance and exhale compassion. Next, think about an experience or feeling that gave you some sense of joy today. Perhaps you spent time with a friend or participated in an activity you love. Notice any sensations that come up in your body when you remind yourself about this joyful feeling. Again, imagine that each time you inhale, you are making space to hold this feeling. Imagine that each time you exhale, you are offering gratitude for this feeling or experience. Take a moment to make space for this feeling. Inhale acceptance and exhale gratitude. Bring your attention back to your breath and body.

What feeling was challenging for you?

....

....

....

....

What feeling or experience provided you with some sense of joy?

....

....

....

....

TODAY, THIS MOMENT, AND TOMORROW

It can be helpful to take a moment to reflect on what happened in the past, how you're feeling in the present, and what you're looking forward to in the future. Finish the sentences below.

Today was

....

....

....

....

....

At this moment, I feel

....

....

....

....

....

I'm looking forward to tomorrow because

....

....

....

....

....

Keep Going with Your Mindfulness Practice!

Congratulations! You've reached the end of the workbook!

Let's take a moment to reflect on your journey with mindfulness so far, starting at the very beginning. Close your eyes and think about the moment you first opened this workbook. You might have been feeling uncertain, or maybe you were feeling excited. You might have been hoping that mindfulness would be helpful for a specific reason, and you set a goal for yourself. Or maybe you just wanted to explore the different exercises and have fun!

Think about flipping through the different chapters. What feelings came up for you as you explored each chapter? Were you able to use what you learned to deal with any situations in your own life?

....

....

....

....

Now that you've made it to the final pages, think about how much you've learned since the first page. You've learned about the magic of mindfulness and how it can help you start your day on the right foot, find your focus, get to know your feelings, and work through your worries. You've also learned how mindfulness can help you stay calm in tough situations, make better decisions, act with kindness toward yourself and others, and end your day on a positive note.

Were any of the chapters especially helpful or even challenging for you? Did anything about your mindfulness journey surprise you? Write about your experience below.

....

....

....

....

Even though you're now at the end of this book, your mindfulness journey will continue. By exploring all the different activities, you've developed more awareness about your feelings, thoughts, and actions. You may have even learned something about yourself you didn't know before!

I hope that the tools and practices you've learned in this book will continue to be useful to you in school and at home, and with your relationships with others. You now know many different ways you can practice mindfulness. Keep using the exercises in this book, or come up with new ones of your own. Be creative! Remember, mindfulness is a practice that helps you become aware of what is happening inside and outside of your body. Mindfulness helps you accept your experience as it is instead of trying to push it away or thinking that it's wrong.

I encourage you to keep doing the mindfulness practices every day. You can turn any moment into a mindful moment by simply asking yourself, *"What do I notice right now?"* By doing this, you'll have curiosity about the world around you and compassion for yourself and others.

I wish you all the best as you set off on the rest of your mindfulness journey!

Resources for Kids

YOGA AND MINDFULNESS CARD DECKS

Yoga and Mindfulness Practice for Children or Teens by Little Flower Yoga
These cards are a perfect way to use mindfulness practices and yoga either at home or on the go. They include many different yoga, meditation, and breathing activities.

Yoga Pretzels: 50 Fun Yoga Activities for Kids and Grownups by Tara Guber and Leah Kalish
These cards are a great way to do mindfulness practices through yoga movement. They give you ideas for different mindful movement and breathing practices.

APPS

Headspace App for Kids
Headspace.com/meditation/kids
You can use this app by downloading it on a phone or tablet (you might need your parents' help!) for fun mindfulness videos and guided meditation practices.

Stop, Breathe and Think App for Kids
StopBreatheThink.com/kids
This app is made for kids just like you, and it suggests specific mindfulness practices based on how you're feeling, which is so cool!

BOOKS

Alphabreaths: The ABCs of Mindful Breathing by Christopher Willard and Daniel Rechtschaffen
This illustrated book offers a playful and fun guide to the power of the breath while introducing the basics of mindful breathing.

I Am Human (A Book of Empathy) by Susan Verde
This beautiful book celebrates the power of empathy and compassion for all parts of yourself and others.

The Mindfulness Coloring Book by Emma Farrarons
This book allows you to do mindfulness practices through making art and mindful coloring, two fun ways to find your focus and calm your body.

This Moment Is Your Life (and So Is This One) by Mariam Gates
This colorful book helps explain the basics of mindfulness and gives you some additional ideas for how to do mindfulness practices on your own.

Resources for Parents, Teachers, and Counselors

WEBSITES

Little Flower Yoga

LittleFlowerYoga.com

Little Flower Yoga provides online and in-person mindfulness facilitator trainings for educators, clinicians, and families.

Mindful Schools

MindfulSchools.org/training/mindfulness-fundamentals

Mindful Schools offers an online training program for educators interested in bringing mindfulness practices into the classroom for children and adolescents.

Stop, Breathe and Think for Educators

StopBreatheThink.com/educators

The Stop, Breathe and Think app provides educators with free access to guided mindfulness activities, yoga, and games for their students.

BOOKS

Everyday Blessings by Jon Kabat-Zinn and Myla Kabat-Zinn

This book provides an introduction to mindful parenting, offering support through various mindfulness practices that can be used within the parenting role.

Growing Up Mindful: Essential Practices to Help Children, Teens, and Families Find Balance, Calm, and Resilience by Christopher Willard

This book shows parents and professionals how to model and teach the skills of mindfulness to youth.

Happy Teachers Change the World: A Guide for Cultivating Mindfulness in Education by Thich Nhat Hanh and Katherine Weare

This book provides an overview of the importance of mindfulness for educators, offering mindfulness practices that teachers can use along the way.

Radical Acceptance by Tara Brach

Integrating mindfulness practice and the power of self-acceptance and nurturing, this book is a beautiful introduction to the power of mindfulness in everyday life.

The Whole Brain Child by Daniel Siegel

This book outlines many mindfulness-based strategies to help nurture a child's developing mind and help the whole family thrive.

Index

Acknowledgments

· · · · · · · · · · · · · · · · · · · ·

I am overwhelmed with gratitude for the opportunity to write this book, and I thank Callisto Media for giving me the opportunity to make this dream come to life.

This book would not have been possible without the support of my family, friends, and loved ones. To Mom, Dad, Kait, Justin, Otis, and Sami, thank you for filling me with light and supporting me each step of the way.

Finally, this project would not have been possible without my students and clients. To be able to hold space for you to be supported, heal, and grow is a true honor. You are the true teachers.

About the Author

· · · · · · · · · · · · · · · ·

Hannah Sherman, LCSW, is a Brooklyn-based licensed clinical social worker and mindfulness educator. As both a school social worker and private practice psychotherapist, she supports children, adolescents, and adults in their journey toward healing and growth.

As a children's yoga and mindfulness teacher, Hannah works to help young people use their bodies and minds as tools to navigate their own experience of the world with curiosity and compassion. Having always honored a holistic lens toward well-being, she is deeply passionate about supporting children in establishing a positive connection to their bodies and feeling empowered by their minds.

Hannah offers education-based and skill-building professional development workshops to helping professionals, including educators and mental health practitioners. She has developed and implemented mindfulness-based programs and curricula for New York City–based schools. Additionally, she provides coaching to caregivers who are interested in bringing mindfulness to their parenting practices.

To learn more about her approach and offerings, visit HannahSherman.com and follow her on Instagram at @HannahShermanTherapy.

CPSIA information can be obtained
at www.ICGtesting.com
Printed in the USA
JSHW012138110422
24811JS00004B/156